A Season's Learning

A Season's Learning

Poems by

Alan Webb

© 2022 Alan Webb. All rights reserved.
This material may not be reproduced in any form, published,
reprinted, recorded, performed, broadcast,
rewritten or redistributed without
the explicit permission of Alan Webb.
All such actions are strictly prohibited by law.

Cover design by Shay Culligan
Cover image by Isuru Ranasingha or Sina Bahar

ISBN: 978-1-63980-187-9

Kelsay Books
502 South 1040 East, A-119
American Fork, Utah 84003
Kelsaybooks.com

Contents

Morning Light	11
A Sunrise	12
Blue Morning	13
Misty Morning	14
Cloudy Day	15
Sunset	16
Starry Night	17
Fireflies on the Rise	18
Old Town Blues	19
Children at Play	20
Lullabies	21
Sun Rain	22
Birds That Fly in the Rain	23
The Aeronautic Dancing Hummingbird	24
Wildflower	25
Spring Cleaning of a Barn	26
Caged Bird	27
A Fallen Nest	28
Strange Clouds	29
Omen	30
Liquor Store Wise Men	31
The 2nd Street Wonder of the World	32
Church on Sunday	33
Cemetery	34
Things Lost in the Fire	35
Summer Rain Storm	36
Storms	37
Home Sweet Home	38
Seasons	39
A Day of Gardening	40
A Nocturnal Affair	41
Moths to the Flame	42
Student of Gravity	43

Lost Hunting Dog	44
Roadkill	45
A Woodland Trail	46
Quell of Day	47
An Approaching Train	48
The Ocean Pier	49
The Beach	50
Highway Voyage	51
Autumn's Palette	52
Fall's Evening Turns to Night	53
The Window	54
The Happening On	55
The River	56
Migrating Birds	57
Snow Storm	58
Cabin Fever	59
Fireside Thoughts	60
Winter Haul	61

Morning Light

Morning mist condenses
And collects on leaves and blades of grass
The coursing air is invigorating and crisp
Providing photosynthesis to the surrounding land
Early birds sing and chirp with profound harmony and glee
Awaken from their nest and homely tree
The radiant sun is rising east
Golden warm and majestic
Piercing rays are caught
And shine upon the water dew's
Glistening reflection
Wind is whispering delicately throughout the region
A perfect start to an imperfect day
A path yet unbeaten

A Sunrise

Something wonderful is rising in the east
As an elegant brilliance makes its peak
In the tree tops over yonder
Is where this presence manifests
Warming, inviting, exquisite spherical golden crest
You can feel it on your eyelids
There is this underlined feeling of exultation
Rising above, making its semblance known
Starting the day anew while setting the tone
Blazoned across the big blue beautiful sky
A true miracle if you have ever seen it with the naked eye
A timeless ritual showing a higher power at hand
We feel it in the depths of ourselves and begin to understand
The world works in mysterious ways
One can't help but give God praise

Blue Morning

Arising promptly are the birds
Who sing their morning song
Beckoning toward the wind
Musical notes and chirps
Announcing nature's glory
And today's unraveling story

Cerulean and violet morning glory
Bloom amongst a hedge's ragged edge
Wet with dew
Open from close
As scores of miniature umbrella heads
A flock of Mourning Doves
Rummage about an earthy plowed field
Then fly away and above with wings fluttering
From there to here

Here it's cool, humid, mild
The sun has arisen and is hidden
Behind a difference of clouds
In which the heat of the day has yet to beguile
The sky's mixture. Parchment and pale blue,
Morning is slowly but surely moving to noon

Misty Morning

A phantom mist hovers and covers the land
Dampening it with a slivery strand
Blotting vision and appearance
As a shapeless, floating mystic
A spotty tranquil light shines through
Giving the setting an odd pale hue
While there's a presence of quietude
Currents of fog move by in slow motion
They walk amid a vast ghostly ocean
Who moves in the twilight of this misty morn?
An opaque vagueness that replaces the dawn

Cloudy Day

A sea stream of white clouds
Coast on the blue skyline for miles
Odd shapes and styles
I find myself envying heaven's light clouds
Their spacious boundary makes me wonder
Where's the beginning, and where do skies end?
Just a sweeping gleam of light
Fills the shadow's in my mind
The wind is whispering a lost parable
Whose translations are hidden
Within the breath of day
A drifting consonance is touching my skin
Then casually moves on, slipping away

Sunset

The sun is setting
On today's memory and forgetting
As it has in days of old
Giving a glittering to the land
Creating a city of sparkling gold
A sacred El Dorado
With outreaching shadows
Stretching out giant hands
Covering the earth like a crystal ball
Forecasting far-reaching mysterious plans
The day's course has closed and runs its span
With the slipping and fading of the red sun
Timely to leave
Timely to come

Starry Night

Starry night in the cosmic firmament high above
Stars are sparkling, twinkling lights beckoning to us
A bluish hybrid raven and indigo sky
Only augment their luminous appeal
Of a galaxy outside a world
Something truly surreal

Soaring night airplanes
Casually mimic shooting stars
Though an aviator's aircraft
Won't fly near where we are
How many stars are in the sky?
Number them if you can
Better off journeying the Sahara Desert
Or counting grains of sand

Timeless, these stars that illuminate the night
North Star has guided our ancestor's plight
Shining an ever sense of nostalgia
Making the present a wonderful gift
And the future is ever more awesome

Fireflies on the Rise

Fireflies are on the rise
Some are far while others draw nigh
Seen glowing in the yard, field low and high
Somewhat drearily lighting the sky

I caught one between my two hands
And held its candlelight vigil
I had to let it go again
A specter of company
Freer now, to go and be

Fireflies weren't meant for a mason jar
They only die and break your heart
A little fallen evening star—
A given sign
A little light—let it shine

Old Town Blues

A reminiscent hue shines down
Over a small humble town
Where the working man wears a crown
Breadwinning days of making rounds
Give way to nights sleepy and sound
Little is known of what tomorrow holds
We embrace it with will and try to hold our own
But can you hear the cries of our inner moans
And the stories that go untold as each new day unfolds
Cozy homes housing families
Slicing a warm homemade pie shared between
Of offered hope and dreams
Tomorrow its back to a daily routine

Children at Play

Unadulterated little balls of verve play outside undisturbed
Oblivious, at least for this moment of a troublesome world
Romping around in the recess of rapture
Out of realities hat, they fabricate magic
Supplied with the tools of make-believe
To them, hope is an awakened dream
From lullabies whispered to them fast asleep
The future resides inside of them as natives of nascent
But in this ephemeral passing, they couldn't be least concerned
About it

Lullabies

A comforting song
To soothe your soul of woes and wrongs
Listen to this whispered psalm
To bid and grant you solace
In the dark of night
Until the light of morning.
Be allayed from all realities harms
Rest your weary eyes
For love is timeless and long
Fear not being weak in these moments
For that is when you are strong
Though the bough may break
And your wakeful date will come
Meditate upon this lullaby
And for now, dream on—

Sun Rain

A vague line is drawn where sun and rain meet
A gathering of rain clouds, a collection of humid heat
This challenge in the sky is a sight to behold
Rain falling in spurts whilst the sun shines amber gold

This rivalry of sorts may have you wonder why?
The results of this phenomenon
Have produced a rainbow emblazoned across the sky
The sky itself has an odd mixture of color
Yellow, orange, a slight pink
Or purple, which accentuate one another

The sun gives the rainfall a magnificent glisten
Like falling caramel cellophane wrappers
Shimmery everywhere in its very appearance
Superstitious folk may be in a fright
And very well wonder whether the devil is beating his wife.

The sun and rain make a quite peculiar pair
You can smell the petrichor on the ground
And wet pavement as it evaporates into the air
It's truly a sight and experience that meshes well together
Making for more enthralling weather

Birds That Fly in the Rain

This spectacle, once seen, gives you inspiration to believe
Birds flying in the rain, on their own wings
The old saying goes, rain falls on the just and the unjust
Watch these animals move through rain and wind gust
Airborne, despite the adversities of nature
Even when odds are not suited to their favor
Gifted with a natural ability and form from their creator
Making their way to the nest which they call home
On the way to safety, no more time to roam
In time the rain will come to cease
Although it makes me wonder about the notion to achieve

The Aeronautic Dancing Hummingbird

Today I saw a hummingbird in a vigorous flight
Going back and forth
And from left to right
It was like this bird was dancing on the wind
And its partner was the flower and nectar within
Exchanging dances with each and every flower
Until it had its fill of sweet devour

Wildflower

Colorful and elusive wildflowers
Bloom across the wilderness
With an expressive texture of gentle tenderness
Grew in merited metamorphosis
With an untamed brilliancy
A natural subsisting art of tranquility
Nurtured by Mother Nature
A plant adorned and tempered
As one of her many auspicious creations

Spring Cleaning of a Barn

A wooden barn red with paint
Sets in backyard quarters
Housing numerous things
On the brink of hoarding
Miscellaneous valuables
Foremost and forgotten
Stored over the years
God only knows how it happened?
It's a season to organize disorder
Before a minimalist catches
The Holy Ghost
And preaches on every corner

Caged Bird

Locked away in bondage grief
To sing a song beckoning free
A release from all bars and confinement
To fly away right into the sky's alignment
Are you the captor, sympathizer, or abolitionist?
Because this bird of nature's measurement,
Surely does not deserve this!
Its song is only half of what it could undoubtedly be
If only allowed to fly and flap and spread its wings
This favor no mere words can express
Liberation always trumps repression
Don't leave it in its blues of melancholy lament
The hour has passed, and the time is spent
Go fly away, bird; your song is your own
A priceless gift that no other can own

A Fallen Nest

An elaborate constructed wren's nest
Has fallen and crumbled to the ground in a mess
Birds look on in distress
The baby birds have died
Before they have learned to fly
In the painstaking time it took
To erect labor and fashion
Only in a moment's notice and error
It all came down, crashing

Strange Clouds

Strange clouds are hovering above
With an approaching wind
Hinting that something is about to begin
You can feel the hair raise on your skin
As sooty slate clouds start to roll in
An ominous presence is making itself familiar
As it gathers and configures
Enough to make your spine feel a shiver
Nature's natural apparition thriller

Omen

This morning a bird flew into our glass screen door
Knocking itself out clean on the front porch
With wings ruffled outspread and a broken head
An unspoken guest at a place of a reception's edge
Leaving on the door a latent taint
A breathy condensation of folly and fate
A fleeting crash move into realties checkmate
Pawn to its own perception
Wearing a death mask of its own reflection
It landed on the welcome mat
With a final greeting—unwelcomed epitaph

Liquor Store Wise Men

The liquor store wise men
May know more than you'll ever know times ten
With intoxication and street knowledge he's adequate
His best friends are common fellows who make ends meet
And he is familiar with all the sidewalks near the street
He tells fables of white- and blue-collar
And problems with no one that wants to solve them
Belching his truth from the bottom of a bottle
He knows the power of a dollar
Tipsy, as the world turns
He drowns away his sorrow
The liquor store scholar will return again
To his oasis in the desert
Or is it a mirage?
Sooner than tomorrow

The 2nd Street Wonder of the World

A plastic grocery bag is pushed and pulled
In the currents of the wind
Going up in gyration while inflating and deflating
Then coming back down again
It moves ceaselessly and easily
Like a jellyfish in the sea
No one stops and stares but only me
It romps around, stopping if only for a pause
A nonbiodegradable tumbleweed tumbling across
Standing out in the backdrop of it all
It pins itself up against a wall
The rustling of the plastic flapping its own kind of talk
Then it blew toward me, bouncing crash for crash
I caught the 2nd street wonder in my hand then kindly put it
In the trash

Church on Sunday

Children of God gather into his house of worship
To offer praise, give thanks, and absorb the pastor's sermon
Brothers, sisters, family members, parents, and guardians
Fill pews and pulpit alike with hearts that are ardent
Choir and band liberate spiritual musical selections
Uplifting souls of the people in every section
Afterward, a prayer of peace, love, and happiness
For healing and protection

Ladies and men are in their Sunday best
Wearing suits and dresses and those infamous hats
A baby cries as a mother slowly rocks them and dries their eyes
Scholarly moment to divulge within the antiquity wisdom
Of biblical scripture
Timeless lessons that instill and remain persistent
As the pastor speaks, we listen
Devotional alter calls followed by a worthy benediction
Hugs are shared along with a joining of hands
A sense of supernatural unity surpassing logic
From the chief in command

Cemetery

Staid tranquility compasses the burial ground
In exception of the call of a Northern Mockingbird
And the carrying of the wind, there is hardly a sound
The ground has a stone crushed paved path
All around is freshly cut green grass
There are graves marked with a headstone inscription
Embellish with flowers and precious mementos
There is the presence of tall mausoleums
A final destination for those laid to rest
Through trials and tribulations
They have succeeded and passed God's test
Countless names of loved ones no longer in the fray
Who have imprinted on our souls
And stay in our hearts and minds each day

Things Lost in the Fire

A house is going up in flames
There's a blaring of a siren as it burns wild and untamed
Outside, family and nearby onlookers watch in vain
Cries arise in dismay
As attempts to put out the fire are made
A firefighter truck pulls up and takes aim
While water gushes out of the water hose
tank to subdue the blaze
There's crackling and splitting of wood that reverberates
Black smoke issues out in rage, then spreads across the way
Calamity has taken the news of the day
The house further disintegrates
Hopes are dashed with the realization it can't be saved
What do you do? What do you say?
When everything you've known as home has come to waste
Negotiating with being displaced and evident heartbreak
Those memories are now charred remains
And nothing will ever be the same.

Summer Rain Storm

Summer rain falls on the window pane
Abrupt water flows down the shutter
Outside the house without restraint
Drips and drops batter along the tin rooftop
Churning rhythmically in the backdrop

The wind howls and blows cool midnight air
Gusty and brisk, down to bear
Past dense clouds that gather in the deep sky
Sketched and painted with black and blue dye

Lightning flashes across the night
Bursting with constant discharges of light
A scene of alarming and thunderous fright

Sharp and drumming against the horizon
An impressive expansion of echoing bass
Then, trailing not too far behind it
Roars like wild lions prowling the sky
In a jungle of firmament, way up high

Storms

I am in the eye of a raging storm
To blind to be saved
Surrounded by a restless stir that continues to wage
A Jerusalem stone is asunder away
My faith is quaked and moved in a mortar
I am a man of clay
To be fashioned and shaped
Fasten to the architecture, remnants of love's fallen frame
I cleave, and I cleave but no longer stay
I possess an endearment for the new break of day
Skies are a vivifying transient gray
In time the surge passes and allays
I walk like a vagabond through lands and remains
Dredging for signs of life
Rationing my hopes for a reverse of blight
Some manifestation to soothe the soul
Storms may come, but soon they will go

Home Sweet Home

It is sure is good to have a home
To have a roof overhead and somewhere to rest my bones
A shelter from the heat
Protection from the storm
And when it's cold, somewhere to keep warm
I often think of less fortunate souls
Who don't have a home and place of their own
It just isn't right and should not be condoned
You see them with signs and disheveled faces
Passing them with their backpacks and cases
Along their way, they've hit rock bottom
With less than a dollar within their pocket
I can't imagine some of the hardships
They may have endured or have been shown
They are society's lost and disowned—
Everybody deserves a home sweet home

Seasons

Seasons come and go on the chariot of time
Merriment and memories all left behind
The renewal of nature cannot be denied
We are a testament to humankind
Bound to our ongoing narratives
As change comes along within our lives
The shape of circles drawn by God
Transcends mathematical understanding
With the grand life cycles of this planet
The seasons are siblings, each one with a trait
Teaching us lessons and guiding our fate

A Day of Gardening

I hold freshly tilled dirt in my hands
May as well have the world within my hands
As it breaks and turns over
The smell is of childhood misadventures and youth
I begin to understand a worm's enthusiasm
Multilayered labyrinths
Mother Nature's soul is deep

A picket fence garden grows in the backyard
Next to an old magnolia tree
There are rows of hot peppers and cherry tomatoes,
Lettuce that's grown from spring
Occasionally phthalo green dragonflies
Spiral around in a hovering spree while I pull weeds
Brown squirrels chatter, leaping from tree to tree
On a branch, there's a stowed away cocoon underneath

The waterer has collected rain to fill it again
Marigolds and pots of purple lavender grow fit
The wind is an emanating scent
Mosquitos' larvae swim in containers and a nearby ditch
The sun's rays permeate and are slowly subsiding
The day is muggy and fair while a crow
And two catbirds territorially
Squawk and dogfight like fighter planes in midair
After much gardening and tending from today's manifest
It's time for a bountiful reap and rest

A Nocturnal Affair

The still night beckons and whispers
A natural instinct with extension
Crickets if the season is right
Have a midnight melodic note
On which I cherish and further dote
Porch lights and street lights glow
It could be warm, cool, or cold
Traffic slows down with cars in the distance
Sacred darkness around below and above in suspension

As if you've entered an umbra
Nature's perfume is heightened and scented
Between hidden limbs of a pine, a spider with a web is spinning
A stray black cat creeps the borders of the yard
In this twilight hour, as the night thins and thickens
Some people are sleeping while time is still ticking
But the ebony cloak cannot remain hidden
Soon the light will gleam, and the sun will rise
So, until it is here, with all its fanfare—
Partake in your nocturnal affair

Moths to the Flame

Something primal and instinctive in this urging allure
A magnetic spectacle with an undeniable pull
This ignited spark has caused a reaction
The light of the fire has a tragic attraction
Moths flying unwarily toward the flame
Victimized mortally scorching their wings
Once burnt, never airborne again
No comforting guidance felt in the wind
Does the moth claim its innocent wings of desire
Flitter unconsciously closer and higher?

Student of Gravity

I want to fly like a butterfly
Free of worry and whose momentary notice
Brightens your day
Unbothered by the guides of fate
My envy is to wing in a similar way
I'm held down by reality's weight
With a balloon full of helium
Tied to invisible fingers of fate
I am teased by hopes and options
Until I find some way to burst and pop
Left with feelings of lethargy
Forever a C-plus student of gravity
And part of Sir Isaac Newton's pity party

Lost Hunting Dog

There was a lost and deserted
Hunting dog trekking on his own
Near the side of the road and forest, alone
Famished, exhausted, carrying on
Orphaned with no owner or home
He may have hunted legendary game
In pastimes
But this present hunt for shelter
Slips his mind
He lifts his almost-human-eyes
Then whimpers, howls, and vainly tries
To seek a human who will only
Not reject or leave him lonely.

Roadkill

A tragedy we see from day to day
As we travel the road, animals caught in the fray
We pass them casually or notice
The grim prey is no longer in motion
Twisted and mangled for all to see
What animal or spirit did it use to be?

Free for a time, but it couldn't escape
The penalty of death and its untimely fate
Was it destiny? Who really knows?
What culprit dealt the fatal blows
And gut-wrenching crushing of their bones?
Now they lie victims of the road
Food for scavengers, buzzards, and crows

A Woodland Trail

The distinct aroma of honeysuckle and pine
Tickle the fancy of your nose
A breath of fresh air eases predilection woes
Alert ivory dragonflies with onyx wings
Circle and coast about the southern breeze

Black crows are cawing robustly from the inner and outer
Sanctuary of the wood
A meaningful message is conveyed and understood
Nature is unique in its form
Like the cries of a baby when it's first born

Earthworms slowly yet somberly inch through the wet soil
Slimy, in their essence,
Tadpoles wiggle and swim
Bleakly striving to emerge from an evaporating water-filled
Ditch, courtesy of precipitation

Offside is a plentitude of trees, overcasting branches,
Thick shrubs, vines, and hollow logs
Fallen deteriorated trees lie here and there
The day is beautiful, the weather is fair

The paths may broaden, narrow, incline, climb
Westward, northward, southward, east
A casual stroll or a course of travail,
Accessible slope or switchback trail

Deer hoof prints are lightly pressed
Near a stagnant puddle beside a brook
Where a whitetail stopped to have a look
Picturesque wildflowers spread on the ground
While zipping bees pollinate, buzzing around.

Quell of Day

The sun is setting on blazed trails
It speaks of the passenger's tale
Warm and looming over the heartfelt
Like a baby, the day is held
After much fuss winding down for a spell
The day was in slow commotion

An assemblage of souls
We live in a restless world
Merchants on the move in the flux of life
Marching to the cadence of zeitgeist

A zephyr blows over a lazy batch of cattails
By an overgrown field that is bare
A far cry compared to a metropolis
A place where there is solace and frenzied paces are quelled

An Approaching Train

A train echoes far off
Coming closer and closer by the minute
A railroad crossing guard comes down
Bells are ringing, and a red light turns ticking
Vibrations are similar to a mechanical monster

You can feel it
Approaching and chugging
Brakes hissing and screeching
Blowing horn hauling freight
Sounding like a wild banshee
Let loose in the distance

The Ocean Pier

You can see the people
On the pier before you approach
The lasting foundations
Of a wooden structure built long ago
The windy sea currents blow
The sea-salt breeze and wooden scent
It hits you as you make your way down the pier

Spaced benches on either side
And those fishing with reels
The sun is sweltering and at a high
Although guided by the wind going by
There's the emitting and prevalent sound
Of water gushing all around

White-greyish seagulls
Screech, perch and fly around the sky
Such a funny-looking flock
Searching for something to find
The blue coast is vast and magnificent
Stretching far and wide, almost infinite
Waves bounce and come in for days on end

The Beach

There's this gritty feeling you get with sand between your toes
The overlay of texture and the way it is composed
Waves consistently crashing coming ashore
Splashing everywhere, making a sonorous roar
You can smell the ocean breeze and sea salt in the air
There are people strolling all along the beach
Sitting nearby with beach towels, umbrellas, and recliner chairs

Overhead planes may circle and pass by with an advertising banner
You can hear the engine in the aircraft making a clamor
People are in beach attire, swimming trunks, and bikinis
The sky is a painted canvas, and the sun is beaming
Kids are playing in the sand, constructing sand castles
People play soccer, volleyball, football, and frisbee

Seashells are scattered all along the beach
There are those who collect them as souvenirs valuing each
In the distance, you can see all types of boats
Bouncing on the waves, they dip, sail and float
The lifeguard is on duty; everyone's safe
Making sure the rules are being followed
And no one is out of bounds, and nothing is out of place
People of all ages having fun in the water
Each one responds differently to a funny kind of disorder
Dudes with boogie boards and surfboards catching waves
Then spontaneously wiping out
Then come up with salt water in their mouth

Couples stroll along the beach sometimes hand in hand
There are those lackadaisically laying on their bellies and back
Hoping to catch the perfect tan
The beach is a perfect getaway experience and sight to behold
When the weather is just right, everything is gold

Highway Voyage

Moving through highway, nights
Where stampeding vehicles on the go
Form a line of white headlights,
And red taillights that flash and glow

Moving in flow
Going to and fro
During the day
To destinations undisclosed
On the road
Making their way up and down the coast

Autumn's Palette

Autumn's come to life right before your eyes
Like a classic oil painting
Or, like the world's largest box of oils that rebelled, escaped,
And danced around then danced around some more
Synonymously melted onto the landscape
With a dab and splash, strokes of coats
Off an artist's palette, God's brush has made paint shine
Shedding of leaves from deciduous trees
The lustrous autumnal colors of foliage
Yellow, orange, green, red, and brown
There's beautiful melancholy poetry in the fall of the leaf
Brown leaves twirl in the wind to an earthly rest
Then hamper and rustle along the ground with a hafts caress
Having a crispy and brittle resonance
While held, they readily break and disintegrate
Tree branches lively sway
There is a steady chill that reels
On your skin, you can feel
Autumn is here

Fall's Evening Turns to Night

There's an abundant smell of cotton in the air, panoramically
Planted and blooming about
Appearing as a languorous sea of new powdered snow

Empty operative tractors
Sit on dusty pathways adjacent to the field
Summer has simmered down and conclusively ended
Fall's harvest season is now here

Just a short way in the distant
Herds of deer, buck, doe, or fawn
Are ruminating, then in seconds, are gone

Overhead is a contrast of purple haze sky
Multiple smooth flying airplanes
In accompaniment with billowy streams passing by

Numerous trees have an equivalence of oversized silhouettes
Shortening by noon, covering the ground creating a shadow's
Depth, noisy nocturnal crickets chirp aloud in a series of unison
Filling ears with synonymous wonder and amusement
The old orange globe is westward, withdrawing from the sky
The evening is cool, simultaneously drifting and approaching night

The Window

A transparent window has my gaze
As I peer out into it, I'm amazed
I don't know what it has to give,
Or from it, what I need to take

The world goes on without me unfazed
I'm taken aback and feel estranged
To be within and be without
I speculate on each account
In a meditative disposition

The Happening On

Today at the stroke of eight, as I went out the door
On the backyard lawn, there
Was a stout young buck walking unaware
Past the herd and in the clear
As I stopped my approach, he became attentive
Then another noticed me around the same time

He raised his head with antlers high in the air and stared
We exchange glances in a silent pause
And couldn't have stood a hundred yards apart
Our thoughts and paths have crossed

I was just as surprised as he—
We both were neither foe nor friend
His confidence matched his demeanor
As he snorted, then galloped off
Back to familiar pastures that were greener

The River

Wind calmly passes across the water
There is a solemn serenity garnered
Geese saunter and gather around the river's edge
Then go honking into the water
Or further down the stream overhead
Ripples look like painted strokes from Claude Monet's hands
Turtles play peek-a-boo in and out of the water with their heads
A muskrat is swimming across the way to land
Fish randomly splash and jump, creating a ripple effect
Catfish, brim, or bass could strike your line
Belly flopping in your boat or on land
If you can get them in time
The day is dwindling slowly
Collecting what I brought and caught
Time to go

Migrating Birds

A shrieking armada of migrating birds flies by
Blackening and blotting out the skyline
On their wings, the wind they ride in stride
Encompassing side by side
As waves of an echelon
In motion and flow
To a place they alone
Seem to know

Snow Storm

Cold translucent icicles drip and form
In alignment with excess around the home
The ground is overlaid in white snow
Temperatures have dropped to below zero
You can hear the gritty crunch and bunch
Underneath your shoes and boots
Of snow as you walk upon
More flakes continue to whirl and hurl downward
From last night's storm

Frigid wind nips your skin
With a complimentary singe
The tree tops are overspread
With more snow overhead
Randomly plummeting to the ground in batches
When weighting branches have broken or are snapping
Black ice coats and sheets the road
There are no cars on the go
The land is barren
It's time to stay in from the cold

Cabin Fever

Cabin fever has settled in
Outside there is a ghostly howl of wild wind
Inside I'm haunted by white walls and claustrophobia
We are maintaining and holding over
Bundled from the Darwinism season of winter
Who in all her beauty and splendor takes no prisoners
At least none accounted for
Stationary behind drawn curtains and shut doors
We are sheltered here, souls in hibernation
Under the cold rule of mother nature
Waiting for a hiatus and the familiar friend of spring
With the return of the promised green
For now, the land is sighing a hymn
Dying to be reborn again

Fireside Thoughts

My thoughts near this fireplace
Are just as shapeless
As the sultry embers
That dance right before my eyes
Venting on its own reconnaissance
Expelling energy to some unfound resolve

Winter Haul

In the wake of the winter solstice
Warmth has lost its golden pulpit
The congregation is divided
In the refuge of residence
Nights reign in still silence
Cold is in complete indulgence

The stir of life's pulsation
Is behind a stark veil of desolation
Outside we are monsters
Breathing clouds of condensation

Frost has coup d'état the morning and midnight landscape
The fallen citadel has evanescent crystals and
Diamonds are custom made
That decorate with a luster as it covers and cascades
The sun surmounts in a noble campaign-breaking day
The cold doesn't take leave only lingers, persists, and wanes

About the Author

Alan Webb is from the small, beautiful town of Rich Square, North Carolina. He spends most of his days reading or writing, with coffee or tea nearby. *A Season's Learning* is his first book.

www.ingramcontent.com/pod-product-compliance
Lightning Source LLC
Chambersburg PA
CBHW030914170426
43193CB00009BA/850